NATURE 👓 WATCH

CHEETAHS
Revised Edition

Dianne M. MacMillan

Lerner Publications Company • Minneapolis

CONTENTS

To my dear friend Hope, who is my inspiration

ACKNOWLEDGMENTS
Thanks to Susan Millard, associate researcher at the San Diego Wild Animal Park; Judy Zeno, education curator at Wildlife Safari; and Dr. Lindsey Phillips, School of Veterinary Medicine at the University of California, Davis. Special thanks to Jack Grisham, general curator at the Oklahoma City Zoological Park and coordinator of the Species Survival Plan

Lerner Publications Company
A division of Lerner Publishing Group, Inc.
241 First Avenue North
Minneapolis, MN 55401

Website address: www.lernerbooks.com

Library of Congress Cataloging-in-Publication Data

MacMillan, Dianne M., 1943-
   Cheetahs / by Dianne M. MacMillan. — Rev. ed.
     p.   cm. — (Nature watch)
   Includes bibliographical references and index.
   ISBN 978-0-8225-9417-8 (lib. bdg. : alk. paper)
   1. Cheetah—Juvenile literature. I. Title.
   QL737.C23M2 2009
   599.75'9—dc22   2008021998

Manufactured in the United States of America
1 2 3 4 5 6 – DP – 14 13 12 11 10 09

A cheetah begins its hunt.

An
Elegant Cat

In the cool early morning, a herd of gazelles moves slowly across the African plain. The animals graze, unaware that on a distant mound two amber eyes watch their every move. Suddenly through the tall grass, a blur of spotted tan fur springs toward the herd. A large cat singles out one of the animals. Although the herd scatters, within seconds, the hunter has caught and killed the gazelle. The large cat is a cheetah, the fastest animal on land.

With long legs, a slender body, and beautiful spots, the cheetah is considered by many to be the most elegant of cats. Cheetahs are members of the cat family, called Felidae. All cats—from "big cats," such as lions, tigers, leopards, and jaguars, to house cats—are part of this family. The cheetah's scientific name is *Acinonyx jubatus.*

The ancestors of the cheetah roamed all over Europe, Asia, North America, and Africa. Many of them lived in what has become known as the Middle East, Pakistan, and northwest India.

One hundred years ago, over 100,000 cheetahs lived in Africa alone. As of the late 2000s, around 12,500 remain, mostly in small areas of southern and eastern Africa. The problem is even more grim in Iran in southwestern Asia. Around 200 cheetahs can be found there. This fascinating animal is in serious danger of becoming **extinct**, or dying out.

 The name *cheetah* comes from the Hindi word *cita*, which means "spotted one." Hindi is the national language of India.

This Indian drawing from the late 1500s shows Akbar the Great *(top right)* hunting with a cheetah *(center)*.

ROYAL SPORT

For centuries, Indian royalty prized cheetahs. One emperor of India, Akbar the Great, kept as many as 3,000 cheetahs for a sport called coursing. The cheetahs were trained to hunt animals in front of an audience. A blindfolded cheetah was taken to an open field where a gazelle was grazing. The blindfold was removed. The cheetah bolted after the prey. The watching crowd cheered the cheetah's lightning speed as it chased down the gazelle.

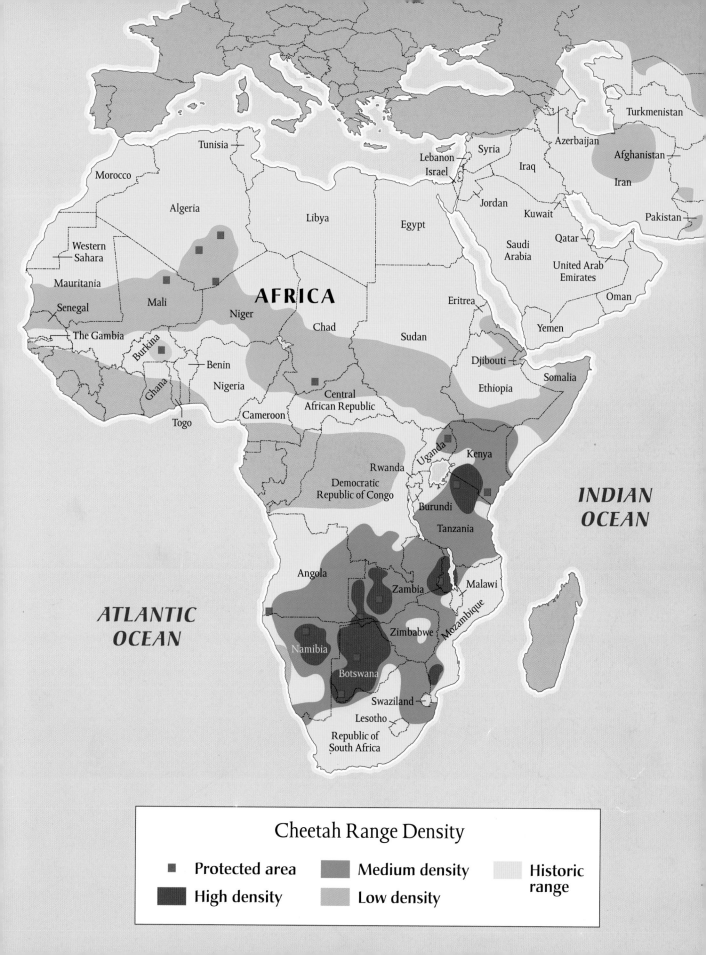

Turkmenistan
Afghanistan
Iran
Pakistan
Tunisia
Lebanon
Israel
Syria
Azerbaijan
Morocco
Iraq
Jordan
Kuwait
Algeria
Libya
Egypt
Qatar
Saudi
Arabia
United Arab
Emirates
Oman
Western
Sahara
Mauritania
AFRICA
Senegal
Mali
Niger
Chad
Sudan
Eritrea
Djibouti
Yemen
The Gambia
Burkina
Benin
Nigeria
Central
African Republic
Ethiopia
Somalia
Ghana
Togo
Cameroon
Uganda
Kenya
Rwanda
Democratic
Republic of Congo
Burundi
Tanzania
INDIAN
OCEAN
Angola
Zambia
Malawi
ATLANTIC
OCEAN
Namibia
Zimbabwe
Mozambique
Botswana
Swaziland
Lesotho
Republic of
South Africa

Cheetah Range Density

■ Protected area

■ High density

■ Medium density

■ Low density

■ Historic
range

SIZE AND WEIGHT

The cheetah is bigger than a house cat but smaller than the big cats. Its coat is a light tan color with black spots. The pattern of spots is different for every cheetah. On its tail, the spots come together to form four to six rings. The tail ends in a bushy white tuft. Its belly is also white.

Cheetahs are easily recognized by their **tear lines**. These are long black stripes that run from the corner of each eye down to the mouth. They look sort of like the marks made when someone has been crying a lot. Scientists think these lines protect the cheetah's eyes from the glare of the sun. Cheetahs hunt during the bright light of day. They rely on their eyesight to find their **prey**.

You might have seen football players with black grease under their eyes. They put it there for the same reason as nature gave the cheetah tear marks—to cut down on the sun's glare.

Top: The black tear lines under a cheetah's eyes help it see in bright sunlight.
Right: The spots on a cheetah turn into rings at the end of its tail.

A cheetah stalks its prey. Cheetahs have very good eyesight. Unlike most cats, they hunt during the day.

A cheetah's short fur looks as if it would be soft, but it actually feels like a coarse brush. The fur that makes up its black spots is longer and softer. Along the back of the neck, the fur forms a **mane** a few inches long. Sometimes the male's mane is longer than the female's. However, a cheetah's mane is still much shorter than a lion's. It also doesn't circle the whole head as a lion's does.

Cheetahs have small heads with short, rounded ears. Compared to big cats, their chests are bigger in relation to the rest of their bodies. Their legs are also much longer than those of other cats. An adult cheetah usually weighs between 100 and 140 pounds (45–64 kg). It stands about 30 inches (76 cm) tall at the shoulder and is about 4 feet (1.2 m) long. Its tail may be 26 to 33 inches (66–84 cm) long. In comparison, a lion might weigh 500 pounds (227 kg) and be 9 feet (2.7 m) long. Cheetah males are usually slightly bigger than females. Overall, though, it's hard to tell male and female cheetahs apart.

A cheetah's mane is barely noticeable on its upper neck area.

This cheetah has just caught some prey—a Cape hare. Cheetahs are smaller than tigers, but they are much bigger than house cats. Cheetahs eat small animals such as hare, as well as larger animals such as antelope.

MADE FOR SPEED

Almost every part of a cheetah's body is made for speed. Its body is slender and light. Its long tail helps it stay balanced. The bones in a cheetah's feet and legs are especially designed to take the pounding of a hard run. Like other cats, they run on their toes. This makes it easier to make sudden turns.

Cheetahs cannot pull in their claws the way house cats and big cats can.

Even the cheetah's claws are designed for speed. They are long, blunt, and very strong. The cheetah is the only member of the cat family whose claws can't **retract**, or pull up inside its paws. With the claws always pushed out, its paws look more like a dog's feet than a cat's. These special claws grip the ground and help the cheetah push off.

Because their claws look a bit like those of a cat and a dog, some people used to think cheetahs were part dog and part cat.

From a standing start, the cheetah can reach 45 miles per hour (72 km/h) in 2 seconds. Most race cars can't get to that speed that fast.

The cheetah's spine, or backbone, works somewhat like a Slinky toy. Its spine helps the cat take long strides. As it runs, its spine bends and straightens, pushing the cheetah forward like a giant spring. For short distances, no animal can match the speed of a cheetah. It can cover as much as 20 feet (6 m) in one stride. It can reach speeds of up to 70 miles per hour (113 km/h). A racehorse at its fastest gallops just over 40 miles per hour (64 km/h). A sprinting cheetah looks as if it is flying across the ground rather than running.

A cheetah's spine bends *(top)* and straightens *(bottom)* as it runs.

A Cheetah's Day

ON A TYPICAL DAY, THE CHEETAH WAKES AT SUNRISE. THE animal stretches its long legs and then slowly stands, arching its back *(above)*. After stretching, it sets off to look for prey. Climbing up on termite mounds or other small hills helps it get a clear view over the flat, grassy **savanna** where it lives.

Keen eyesight helps cheetahs spot their prey from as far as 3 miles (4.8 km) away. Like all cats, they are **carnivores**, or meat eaters. They hunt small- and medium-sized animals such as antelope, impalas, rabbits, game birds, and young ostriches.

When the heat of the day becomes too much for a cheetah, it finds shade in which to rest. Even when it's very hot, cheetahs don't drink much water. They get most of their water from the meat they eat. On

A group of cheetahs rests in the shade.

occasion, they drink from water holes or rivers, but amazingly, they can go for up to 10 days without water.

In late afternoon, after the weather has cooled down, the cheetah resumes its patrol. Unlike big cats, the cheetah is **diurnal**, or active during the day. At night, it is usually sleeping or resting in one place.

HOME RANGE

Cheetahs do not have a permanent home, or den. Each year, most cheetahs migrate, or travel, over a large area. They follow grazing herds of gazelles, impalas, and other hoofed **mammals**. Cheetahs

A cheetah takes a drink from a river.

15

Archaeologists unearthed this cheetah head in the tomb of Egyptian king Tutankhamen.

When a cheetah sits on its haunches and stares across the plain, its lean body resembles an ancient Egyptian statue. In fact, rich ancient Egyptians kept cheetahs as pets. A golden figure of a cheetah, with its tear lines, was in the tomb of the Egyptian king Tutankhamen.

travel the same area year after year, covering as much as 40 square miles (104 sq. km). Females live alone except when they have babies, called **cubs**. If a female is walking across the plain and sees another female, she will turn her head and look the other way. Females avoid all contact with one another.

A female cheetah leads her babies across the savanna at midday.

Three male cheetahs watch for prey on the savanna. Male cheetahs sometimes live in small groups, but female cheetahs live alone except when they are raising their young.

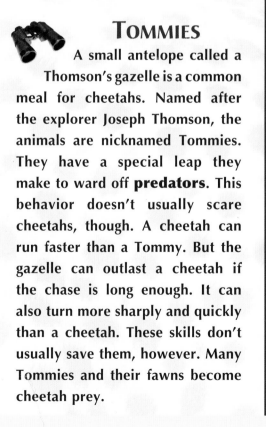

TOMMIES

A small antelope called a Thomson's gazelle is a common meal for cheetahs. Named after the explorer Joseph Thomson, the animals are nicknamed Tommies. They have a special leap they make to ward off **predators**. This behavior doesn't usually scare cheetahs, though. A cheetah can run faster than a Tommy. But the gazelle can outlast a cheetah if the chase is long enough. It can also turn more sharply and quickly than a cheetah. These skills don't usually save them, however. Many Tommies and their fawns become cheetah prey.

Males live alone or with a small group called a **coalition**. Often the members of a coalition are brothers. Males in these groups are usually healthier than lone males, because they have more success at hunting. Two or more males hunting together are able to hunt larger prey such as young giraffes, buffalo calves, or zebras.

Coalitions choose an area, called a **territory**, to call home. They hunt animals that wander into that area. To mark their territory, they spray **urine** on trees and rocks. The smell tells other male cheetahs to stay out. Males that dare to enter a coalition's territory are chased out or sometimes even attacked and killed. A female passing through the area is ignored unless she is ready to mate.

The Swift Hunter

WITH ITS EXCELLENT EYESIGHT, A CHEETAH SPOTS ITS PREY in the distance. It lowers its head, a sign that the hunt is on. The cheetah moves slowly forward. Its eyes stay fixed on its prey. The cheetah's golden coat blends in with the tall grass. Sometimes the only clue that the cheetah is coming is the white tuft on the end of its tail. The tuft appears high above the grass. If the prey seems nervous or senses danger, the cheetah will freeze in place. It stays still until the prey animal relaxes and begins to graze again.

In Action

Finally, when the cheetah is within 300 to 550 feet (92–168 m) of its prey—the length of one or two football fields—it springs into action. As the cat bounds through the grass, the startled animal begins to run. The cheetah is a blur of motion as it stretches out its long body and tail. Within seconds, the cheetah catches up to the fleeing animal. With a front paw, it strikes the animal on the rump. On the inside of the cheetah's foreleg is a claw called a **dewclaw**. This sharp, curved claw hooks the victim and helps knock it over.

As the animal crashes to the ground, the cheetah clamps its jaws down on the animal's throat, cutting off the air supply. The animal is often larger than the cheetah. But it doesn't have time to struggle or kick off the cheetah. The prey animal is gasping for air from the chase. In just a few seconds, the animal stops breathing and dies. The whole hunt and kill may take as little as 20 seconds.

The cheetah's speed makes it hard for an animal to get away. But surprisingly, the animal would have a better chance if it were to just stand still. Cheetahs hunt by singling out one animal and chasing it down. If the animal didn't run, it would have the strength to withstand a swipe on the rump and fight off the cheetah.

Still, cheetahs don't catch every animal they go after. Their speed makes them tire quickly. In a long chase, sometimes they have to give up. They are successful only about one time out of two tries. However, cheetahs are more successful than big cats. They succeed only about one time out of three tries.

A cheetah catches a gazelle. Cheetahs are more often successful when their prey tries to run away. If the gazelle or antelope stands still, the cheetah is too small to kill it.

A cheetah drags an impala to a safer place to eat it.

FEEDING TIME

After the cheetah kills its prey, it drags the victim to an area hidden by bushes or trees. The cheetah doesn't want vultures or other predators to find the kill. Exhausted from the short but rapid chase, it sits and pants like a dog. Its chest heaves with each breath. Finally rested, the cheetah eats quickly, tearing off huge hunks of meat and gulping them down.

The cheetah will need 20 to 30 minutes to catch its breath before it can eat. In this time, other predators can smell the freshly killed animal.

Several times, it will stop between bites and look around for other predators. If a mother cheetah and her cubs are eating together, they position themselves around the dead animal in a star formation. Each one can reach the kill without quarreling.

Three cheetahs sit in a star pattern around their kill so they don't have to fight one another to reach the meat.

The eating habits of cheetahs are different from those of big cats. A cheetah gorges itself on its kill. When its stomach is full, the cheetah walks away. It doesn't care how much food is left. In contrast, lions guard their kill for several days. Tigers come back later for a second helping. Leopards drag their kill up into a tree for safekeeping and a midnight snack. Cheetahs eat only fresh kill. And unlike the big cats, cheetahs rarely eat anything they haven't killed themselves.

The fact that cheetahs eat only what they kill might be helping cheetahs survive. Humans sometimes use traps with meat as bait to catch wild animals. But cheetahs aren't tempted by the meat. They ignore the bait.

Right: This leopard dragged its kill into a tree to keep other predators from stealing it. The leopard will come back to the meat and eat all of it.
Below: Cheetahs eat only fresh meat. They have to be on the lookout for another predator that might try to steal their kill.

Above: **Vultures approach a group of cheetahs as they eat their kill.** *Below:* **A cheetah will walk away rather than fight vultures or strong animals, such as lions or hyenas.**

Often before a cheetah has finished its meal, a lion or a pack of hyenas or a group of vultures will steal the cheetah's food. With weak jaws and blunt claws, the cheetah can't defend itself against more powerful animals. At first sight of a lion or hyena, it lowers its head and backs off. Even a group of vultures will scare a cheetah away. The cheetah's superior speed and hunting skills have produced dinner for other animals. The hungry cheetah will have to try again. It may have to hunt for 2 or 3 more days before making another kill. This is particularly hard for a mother trying to kill enough food to feed her cubs.

CHEETAH
BABIES

CHEETAHS MATE AND GIVE BIRTH TO CUBS THROUGHOUT the year. They don't have a special breeding season. Seven to fourteen days before the female is ready to mate, her urine takes on a special scent. When she urinates on trees and rocks in her area, she lets males know she will be ready to mate soon.

The time during which a female is able to mate, called **estrus**, lasts for 1 week. The **dominant** male in the area, who is larger and stronger than the other males, follows the scent and finds the female. The male and female sniff one another and stay together for a few hours or a day. When the female is ready, she allows the male to mount her.

After the cheetahs mate, the male leaves. If the female does not become pregnant, she will go into estrus again in 10 days. If she does become pregnant, her cubs will be born in about 3 months. When she is ready to give birth, she finds a quiet spot hidden by rocks or bushes. She lies down on her side, and the cubs are born.

CHEETAH MOMS

A cheetah mother takes good care of her cubs. As soon as they are born, she nestles them close to her to keep them warm. The cubs are blind and helpless. But they can find their mother's nipples to nurse. Her milk is the cubs' first food.

Cheetahs may have one to eight cubs at a time. A group is called a litter. The average litter has three or four cubs. Newborns weigh from 8 to 10 ounces (227–284 g).

Males and females have no contact other than for mating. Males do not help raise or protect the cubs.

Top: A male and a female cheetah engage in courtship behavior before mating. *Bottom*: A cheetah mom nurses her cubs underneath bushes to keep them hidden from predators.

Cheetah mothers move their cubs on a regular basis to keep them safe.

From the moment of birth, cubs face the constant threat of predators. Mother cheetahs have a big job trying to keep the cubs safe. Every 3 or 4 days, a mother will move her newborn litter to a new hiding spot.

In a 6-week period, one observer noted that a mother cheetah moved her cubs more often than average—21 times. In spite of her protection, one cub was eaten by a leopard.

She carries each cub by the back of the neck, the same way a house cat carries her kittens. Predators are less likely to find the cubs by their scent if they have not been in the same spot for long.

At 5 to 10 days old, the cubs open their eyes and begin to crawl around. Their mother calls them by making low, birdlike chirping sounds. The cubs answer with shrill, high-pitched chirps. After 3 weeks, the cubs are able to walk and follow after their mother. While she is hunting, the cubs hide quietly nearby. Any noise would attract the attention of predators.

GROWING UP CHEETAH

The heads, necks, and backs of the newborns are covered with a furry coat called a **mantle**. The mantle is about 3 inches (7.5 cm) long. It is grayish white on the ends and black closer to the skin. The long hair makes the cubs look bigger and less helpless to predators. Their coloring may help them blend into the shadows.

When the cubs are between 8 and 12 weeks old, they begin to lose their black-and-white mantles. In a few months, they will have full, spotted coats. Their spotted coats help them blend into the tall grass. But they are still in constant danger from predators. Lions, hyenas, leopards, and other animals will eat the cubs if they have the chance.

At about 2 weeks, tiny teeth grow in. At 4 weeks, the cubs begin to eat some meat that their mother brings to them. Their adult teeth will grow in at 10 to 14 months.

Some scientists think a cub's mantle **mimics**, or looks similar to, the honey badger *(left)*, a fierce animal that most predators avoid. A predator who has had a run-in with a honey badger may think twice about preying on a cheetah cub.

Right: These young cubs still have their mantles. Some scientists think the mantles help scare off predators by making the cubs look like honey badgers.

From about 6 months on, the cubs eat only meat. The mother tries to make one kill every day to feed them. As the cubs grow older, the mother teaches them how to hunt for themselves. At first, they watch her. Later, she will bring them small animals that are still alive. The cubs must learn exactly where to bite an animal's throat to kill it. If they miss the throat, the animal will get away. It could harm them with its horns or hooves. Cubs don't hunt on their own until they are about 18 months old.

PLAYTIME AND GROOMING

When not learning how to hunt, cubs spend their days playing. They chase one another's tails and stalk their mother's feet. They play like kittens, tumbling, wrestling, and rolling over and over in the grass. They pounce on one another in a cheetah game of leap-frog. This playing helps develop strong muscles and teaches them skills they will need to survive. Sometimes their mother joins in.

Three cheetah cubs wrestle. Playing and pouncing prepares cheetah cubs for life as adult cheetahs.

A cheetah cub pounces playfully on its mom's head.

A cheetah mother grooms her cub. Teaching her cubs to groom themselves and one another is an important part of preparing them to live on their own.

Grooming or cleaning is an important part of a cheetah's life from an early age. Like all cats, cheetahs have long, rough tongues covered with tiny **rasps**, or hooks. When the cheetah licks its coat, the rasps comb through the hairs to remove dirt, grass, and loose fur. Cheetahs spend many hours every day grooming. A mother and her cubs help one another with the task. Particularly after eating, they all pitch in to make sure everyone's face is clean. At the same time, they purr noisily—almost like a house cat but at a much greater volume! Their purring can be heard up to 20 feet (6 m) away. Cheetahs purr loudest while grooming one another and while resting. Purring is a way of communicating coziness and friendship to one another.

CHEETAH SOUNDS

Scientists don't really know how cats purr. They do know that cats have two sets of vocal chords. Each set produces different sounds. Scientists believe the purring sound is made when the blood flow increases near the upper vocal chords. The sound of the flowing blood is made louder by the air the cat is breathing in and out.

Cheetahs cannot roar, as big cats do. If a hyena or a human tries to steal her family's food or come close to her cubs, a female will moan and growl. She may also lunge forward and stamp her feet on the ground. She raises the hair on her shoulders and neck to make herself look larger. But all of this is a bluff to frighten the animal or person away from her cubs. Solitary cheetahs are usually gentle animals. However, male cheetahs in a coalition have been known to fight to the death an intruder who enters their territory.

When the cubs are between 16 and 18 months old, the mother leaves to mate again and raise a new litter. She has protected her cubs and taught them as much as she can. They will have to survive on their own. The cubs stay together for a few more months. Then the females leave. The male cubs may remain together for life. Or they too may strike out on their own.

The fully grown cubs are able to mate. However, they usually wait until they are older. First-time mothers are usually 2 years old. Males might wait longer than 2 years if older and more dominant males are in the area.

A cheetah growls and raises the hair on her back to scare off an intruder.

THE VANISHING CHEETAH

THE FUTURE OF CHEETAHS IS UNCERTAIN. HUMANKIND IS running out of time to save these elegant cats. In the near future, no cheetahs may be left in the wild. Cheetahs are dying at a faster rate than they can be born. The present life span of a cheetah in the wild is a brief 7 years. Even though females breed frequently, only one in three cubs reach the age of 2 years.

HUMAN DANGERS

The greatest single threat to cheetah survival is loss of **habitat**—the savannas where they live. In countries where cheetahs live, the human population is exploding. To feed the growing numbers of people, more land is needed to grow crops for food. Large areas of the savannas are being divided up and fenced off for farmland and pastures.

As farms are built, antelope, impalas, young ostriches, and other animals that make up the cheetah's diet are moving away. But cheetahs can't move with them. They need wide-open areas to chase down their kill. So they stay on the savannas, where less food is available. Cheetahs and other predators are competing for the same prey. Cheetahs may hunt rabbits, birds, lizards, and frogs instead. They may also kill cattle and other farm animals. Understandably, this is hard on the farmers. In some countries, farmers shoot cheetahs to protect their livestock. This reduces the number of cheetahs even more.

Poachers, or illegal hunters, are another problem facing cheetahs. Poachers kill cheetahs and sell their skins at high prices. Most skins are made into expensive fur coats. Some people also hang cheetah skins on their walls or use them to cover pillows. As cheetahs become more scarce, their skins become more valuable. International laws are supposed to protect cheetahs. But hundreds of the cats still die this way each year.

Above: Herders watch over their cattle on the savanna.
Opposite: A cheetah sits in the tall grass of the savanna. The two biggest threats to cheetahs are loss of habitat and poaching.

PROTECTION EFFORTS

To protect cheetahs from poachers, some areas have been set aside as wild animal parks, or **reserves**. Serengeti National Park and Masai Mara Game Reserve are parks in Tanzania and Kenya that are trying to help the plight of cheetahs. The Cheetah Conservation Fund (CCF) operates a study center in northern Namibia that also educates farmers about them.

However, even on the reserves, cheetahs are not safe if large numbers of big cats are around. They eat cheetah cubs and steal cheetah kills. Cheetahs have always faced this risk. However, with the number of cheetahs and the amount of available food going down, the situation has become more serious.

Dr. Laurie Marker *(far right)*, **the founder of the Cheetah Conservation Fund, educates a group of Namibian schoolchildren about cheetahs at the CCF reserve.**

DR. LAURIE MARKER: CHEETAH CHAMPION

Little did Laurie Marker know that when she moved to Oregon in 1972, she was on a path to become a cheetah expert. She started working at Oregon's Wildlife Safari. She became fascinated by the animal park's cheetah population. She read everything she could find and started making notes. Over time, she was put in charge of the park's cheetahs.

Meanwhile, scientists were trying to figure out why the number of cheetah cubs born in zoos was low. They took blood and sperm samples and studied them. They also looked to the most successful breeding programs. This brought them to Laurie Marker. Wildlife Safari had more than 30 park-born cubs. By the late 1980s, the park had more than 100.

Marker came to realize cheetahs were in grave danger of becoming extinct. She sold all she owned and moved to Namibia in southern Africa. In this sparsely populated country, wildlife and farms are on the same land. She found that farmers were killing cheetahs because they thought they preyed on their livestock. Marker spent years collecting data. She showed farmers that cheetahs can't kill fully grown livestock, only newborns. Cheetahs also give up if they are scared away by big, noisy animals. She suggested the farmers protect their newborns with fierce-sounding donkeys. Slowly, the farmers came around. They were killing fewer cheetahs.

At the same time, Marker got the money to buy 100,000 acres (40,470 hectares) of land in Namibia. She set up the nonprofit Cheetah Convervation Fund, as well as a safe haven for orphaned cheetah cubs. She also began educational and scientific programs. Her studies showed that female cheetahs choose their mates, not the other way around. Following her findings, managers of zoos started setting aside a female with all the males, instead of putting all the females and males together. More zoo-born cubs was the result.

Marker introduced farmers to the idea that special guard dogs would be better protectors of livestock. She started breeding the dogs. Marker's work has helped farmers and wildlife find a way to live together. CCF has stretched into other African countries that have cheetahs. It trains teachers and scientists and even encourages tourism. As one farmer put it, "Laurie saw the bigger picture. [She said] the whole world was going to know about the cheetahs. And it does."

A zookeeper holds a litter of 2-day-old cheetah cubs. Keepers at the San Diego Zoo in California took over the care of the cubs after the mother stopped caring for them.

The future of cheetahs may be in zoos. In zoos, the cheetah's life span is between 12 and 17 years. If they lived that long in the wild, each female would be able to raise as many as six litters of cubs during her life.

But for cheetahs, life in zoos has been difficult too. Cheetahs don't breed well in captivity. Females do not come into estrus as often as they do in the wild. And scientists have discovered that 70 to 75 percent of the **sperm**, or male reproductive **cells**, are weak in males both in zoos and in the wild. This may prevent successful breeding. Sometimes, the zoo-born cubs are not well cared for by their mothers. Then the cubs must be hand-raised by humans, or they will die.

GENETIC PROBLEMS

Before 1956, only one birth of a captive cheetah was recorded. As scientists learn more about cheetahs, more cubs are being born in captivity. But fewer than half of all zoos that have tried to breed cheetahs have succeeded.

Why is breeding in captivity hard for cheetahs? Scientists are studying how cheetahs live and reproduce in the wild. The studies are focusing on **genes**. Genes are found in all cells. They serve as a pattern for any new cells that are made. Genes determine everything about an animal—including its pattern of spots, its size, and its general health. Genes from both parents are passed on to their offspring. Genes usually make every animal just slightly different from either of its parents.

But scientists have discovered that the genes of cheetahs in captivity and in the wild are almost identical. This means that no slight differences exist in the **species**, or kinds, no matter where the animal lives. Over 10,000 years ago, probably four different species of cheetahs roamed Earth. Then something caused almost all of the cheetahs to die. Three of the four species vanished completely. Modern cheetahs are all related to the one species, *Acinonyx jubatus*, that survived. Because of this, fewer than 1 percent of a cheetah's genes are different from another cheetah. In contrast, other cats differ by 21 percent. Humans vary by 32 percent.

Slight differences are needed within a species. They allow animals to grow stronger and to avoid disease. The differences in genes allow some animals of a species to adapt, or change, to deal better with changes around them. For example, if the climate grows colder, animals with longer fur are more likely to survive. They can raise offspring. Those babies will have longer fur too and so will their offspring. In another case, if a food source is taken away, animals might adapt by changing what they eat. They will be more likely to survive. They can teach their young to eat the new foods. They will more likely survive than animals who don't change their eating habits and go hungry.

There isn't much difference among the genes of these three cheetahs, whether they are related or not.

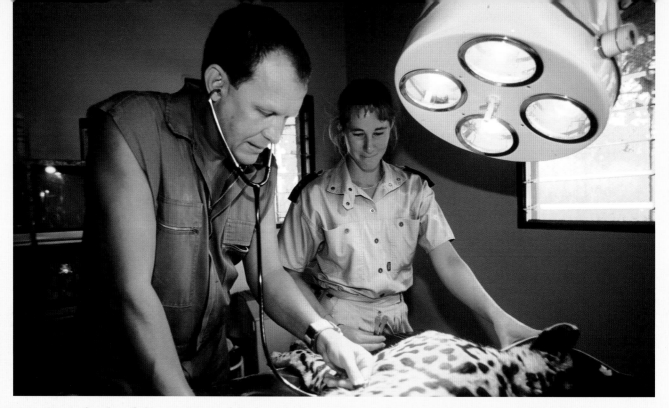

A veterinarian *(left)* examines a sick cheetah. Researchers and conservationists are working to diversify cheetah's genes to make the cats stronger.

Animals that have similar genes tend to respond to changes around them in the same way. If one cheetah is unable to fight illness or adapt to a changing climate, many others probably won't adapt either. Thus the species dies out or becomes more likely to get sick.

In 1982, more than half the cheetahs living in Oregon's Wildlife Safari died from a serious cat disease. The group of animals did not have enough variation in their genes. If they did, some of them might have been able to resist the illness.

WORKING TOGETHER

In the wild, females mate with the strongest and most dominant male. Zoos have fewer cheetahs and fewer choices. This is the greatest challenge for scientists trying to save the cats. Zoos in North America are working together to give cheetahs a better chance for survival. As part of the Species Survival Plan (SSP), zoos keep records of parents and their offspring. They want to breed animals that are as distantly related as possible. This will result in more variation in the offspring's genes.

The SSP also makes sure the healthiest cheetahs mate with one another. Veterinarians and zookeepers pay close attention to the animals' diet, stress, and behavior. They watch carefully anything that can affect cheetahs' ability to reproduce and to live longer.

Several zoos have had some success. Both Wildlife Safari and the San Diego Wild Animal Park in California have had over 100 cheetahs born in their parks since 1970. Other successful breeding programs are located at the Columbus Zoo in Ohio, the Saint Louis Zoo in Missouri, the White Oak Conservation Center in Florida, and the Fossil Rim Wildlife Center in Texas. Scientists hope that someday some of the offspring of captive cheetahs can be returned to the wild, if there is any wilderness left.

This cheetah gave birth to four cubs at the National Zoo in Washington, D.C.

WORKING WITH FARMERS

To protect those cheetahs left in the wild, **naturalists** in Africa are working with farmers to find ways for the farmers to live peacefully with the cats. The naturalists are encouraging farmers to use dogs or donkeys, instead of guns, to scare off the cats and protect their cattle.

Another option for farmers is to catch cheetahs rather than shoot them. In Namibia, the Cheetah Conservation Fund moves these captured animals to reserves in other countries in southern Africa. The wild cheetahs are carefully checked out by veterinarians. If the males are strong and healthy, sperm is collected and sent to zoos in the United States to add variety to their breeding programs. Then the animals are returned to the reserves.

Some of these efforts are showing positive results. For the first time in many years, the cheetah population in Kenya seems to be holding steady. The population in Namibia has increased slowly. Scientists hope these trends will continue.

Laurie Marker stands with rescued orphaned cheetahs at the CCF in Namibia.

ANATOLIAN SHEPHERD GUARD DOGS

Cheetahs are not very brave. If an animal growls or barks loudly at them, the cat will likely go away. Cheetahs also don't usually attack large, fierce-sounding animals. Research on these behaviors gave scientists an idea.

For thousands of years, shepherds in Turkey have been using Anatolian shepherd dogs to guard their sheep from wolves. These guard dogs are large, and they have a fierce, nasty-sounding bark. The Cheetah Conservation Fund has been introducing Namibian farmers to Anatolian shepherd dogs. Farmers use the breed to guard their herds *(below)*. So, instead of farmers shooting cheetahs for preying on their goats or cattle, the guard dogs scare them away.

The vanishing cheetah is in its final race. But it is not racing against a gazelle or a wildebeest. This time, it is racing against extinction. If the cheetah loses the race, then all nature will feel the loss. Lions, leopards, hyenas, jackals, vultures, and other animals that depend on the hunting skills of the cheetah will suffer. Other species of animals and even plants will be affected.

We must find a way to halt the widespread destruction of savannas without denying countries their right to grow food. Cheetahs must be protected until scientists can help this declining species grow strong once more. Governments, scientists, zoos, and people everywhere working together can help this magnificent cat win the race. When future generations see a golden streak sprinting across the savanna, they will know it is the cheetah, the fastest animal on land.

KIDS WHO ARE HELPING SAVE CHEETAHS

Kids throughout the world love cheetahs. But what can a kid do to help save these beautiful animals from dying out? Get creative! By raising money to support cheetah studies and programs that educate farmers and patrol reserves, kids can make a difference. Some kids have made money by being sponsored in races to save the cheetahs. For each mile they race, they are given money they can donate. Other kids have made goods to sell, such as jewelry or cookies. Some kids even use birthday parties as a way to raise money. Instead of getting a gift, they ask guests to give that money to help cheetahs. With the money, kids can adopt cheetahs and cubs being taken care of through groups such as the Cheetah Conservation Fund or the World Wildlife Fund. See what creative ways you can think of to raise money to help cheetahs!

A cheetah gazes over the savanna. With humans moving into their habitat, cheetahs are dying. Their usual prey is moving to areas with fewer people.

A cheetah sprints across the savanna.

GLOSSARY

carnivores: animals that eat meat

cells: the smallest units of life. Genes are made up of millions of cells.

coalition: a small group of two to four male cheetahs—often brothers—that live together

cubs: baby cheetahs

dewclaw: a long, curved claw that is used to help hook and knock over prey

diurnal: active during the day

dominant: the strongest and most powerful animal in an area

estrus: a weeklong period during which a female cheetah is able to become pregnant

extinct: having no members of a species left alive

genes: tiny units in the cells of living things. Genes determine the traits that offspring will get from their parents.

habitat: the type of environment in which an animal lives

mammals: animals that have hair or fur and produce milk to feed their young

mane: a section of longer fur on the back of the neck

mantle: a furry, grayish white and black coat that grows on a cub's head, neck, and back

mimic: to develop the coloring, habits, or body structure of another species

naturalists: scientists who study animals and plants

poachers: illegal hunters

predator: an animal that hunts and eats other animals to survive

prey: an animal that a predator catches to eat

rasps: tiny hooks on a cat's tongue

reserve: a piece of land set aside for wildlife that is off-limits to hunters

retract: to pull up or back inside

savanna: a flat, grassy area in a hot, dry climate

species: a group of animals that are so closely related they can breed with one another. Cheetahs belong to the species *Acinonyx jubatus*.

sperm: male reproductive cells

tear lines: dark lines in a cheetah's fur that run from the inner edge of its eyes down to the corners of its mouth

territory: an area claimed as one's home and defended from other animals

urine: liquid waste that animals pass out of their bodies

SELECTED BIBLIOGRAPHY

Adamson, Joy. *The Spotted Sphinx.* New York: Harcourt Brace & World, 1969.

Amman, Katherine, and Karl Amman. *Cheetah.* New York: Arco Publishing, 1985.

Arnold, Caroline. *Cheetah.* New York: Morrow Junior Books, 1989.

Burnham, Laurie. "Off and Running." *Scientific American*, 258 (February 1988).

Caro, Tim. "An Elegant Enigma." Wildlife Conservation, 99. no. 3 (May/June 1996).

Clutton-Brook, Juliet. *Eyewitness Books Cat.* London: Dorling Kindersley, 1990.

Conklin, Gladys. *Cheetahs: The Swift Hunters.* New York: Holiday House, 1976.

Conniff, Richard. "Cheetahs Ghosts of the Grasslands" *National Geographic*, 196, no. 6 (December 1999).

Eaton, Randall L. *The Cheetah Natures's Fastest Racer.* New York: Dodd, Mead & Co. 1981.

Gugliotta, Guy. "Rare Breed." *Smithsonian Magazine*, 38, no. 12 (March 2008).

Herbison Frame, George W. and Lory. "The Cheetahs In a Race for Survival" *National Geographic*, 157, no. 5 (May 1980).

Kuenkel, Reinhard. "Cheetahs: Swift Cats of the Serengeti." *Geo Collectors Edition,* 1 (1979).

National Audubon Society. *On the Edge of Extinction: Panthers and Cheetahs.* VHS. Atlanta: Turner Program Services, 1989.

Pennise, Elizabeth. "Cheetah Countdown." *Science News,* 144 (September 25, 1993).

Schick, Alice. *Serengeti Cats.* New York: J. B. Lippincott Co., 1977.

Simon, Seymour. *Big Cats.* New York: Harper Collins, 1991.

Starkweather, Helen. "Saving the Cheetah." *Smithsonian.com*. March 2008. http://www.smithsonianmag.com/science-nature/cheetah-interview.html?c=y&page=2 (June 9, 2008).

Stone, Lynn M. *The Cheetah.* Vero Beach, FL: Rourke Enterprises, 1989.

WEBSITES

Cheetah Conservation Fund

http://www.cheetah.org

This site has tons of information about how you can help protect cheetahs and what kids around the world are already doing.

For Kids Who Love Cheetahs

http://cheetahkids.com

Created by a boy named Cameron Carver who loves cheetahs, this site supports the work of the Cheetah Conservation Fund and the National Zoo. It has lots of information that shows kids ways they can make a difference in keeping cheetahs from extinction.

National Zoo/African Savanna

http://nationalzoo.si.edu/Animals/AfricanSavanna

This site is run by the National Zoo and the Smithsonian Institution in Washington, D.C., and explores the many animals, including cheetahs, that live in the grasslands of Africa. It also has a specific section devoted to cheetah conservation.

FURTHER READING

Claybourne, Anna. *Cheetah: Habitats, Life Cycles, Food Chains, Threats*. Milwaukee: Raintree, 2003.

Harkrader, Lisa. *The Cheetah*. Berkeley Heights, NJ: Myreportlinks.com Books, 2005.

Johnson, Julia. *The Cheetah's Tale*. London: Stacey International Publishers, 2004.

Markert, Jenny. *Cheetahs*. Mankato, MN: Child's World, 2006.

Nagada, Ann Whitehead. *Cheetah Math: Learning about Division from Baby Cheetahs*. New York: Henry Holt, 2007.

Squire, Ann O. *Cheetahs*. Danbury, CT: Children's Press, 2005.

Thompson, Sharon Elaine. *Built for Speed*. Minneapolis: Twenty-First Century Books, 1998.

Von Zumbusch, Amelie. *Cheetahs*. New York: PowerKids Press, 2007.

INDEX

ABOUT THE AUTHOR

Dianne M. MacMillan has always been fascinated by the speed and elegance of cheetahs and by their long association with humans. She hopes that this book will encourage young readers to continue the fight to save cheetahs from extinction. MacMillan is a former elementary school teacher with numerous children's books and magazine articles to her credit. She lives in California.

PHOTO ACKNOWLEDGMENTS

The images in this book are used with the permission of: © Royalty-Free/CORBIS, all page backgrounds, pp. 1, 5, 13 (bottom), 14, 18, 24, 32, 35, 43, 44, 45, 46, 47, 48; © James Warwick/Riser/Getty Images, pp. 2-3; © Gerry Lemmo, pp. 4, 8 (top left), 10, 14, 32; © age fotostock/SuperStock, pp. 5, 8 (bottom right), 13 (top), 20, 24; © Victoria & Albert Museum, London/Art Resource, NY, p. 6; © Laura Westlund/Independent Picture Service, p. 7; © Andy Rouse/The Image Bank/Getty Images, p. 9; © Tom Brakefield/SuperStock, p. 11; © Suzi Eszterhas, www.eszterhasphotography.com pp. 12, 15 (bottom), 16 (bottom), 19, 25 (bottom left), 26, 27 (bottom), 29, 30, 34, 40, 41, 42; © Fred Bruemmer/Peter Arnold, Inc., p. 15 (top); © Robert Harding/Robert Harding World Imagery/Getty Images, p. 16 (top); © Daryl Balfour/Riser/Getty Images, p. 17; © James Warwick/The Image Bank/Getty Images, p. 18; © Ken Dyball/Photographer's Choice RR/Getty Images, p. 21; © Fritz Polking/Visuals Unlimited, p. 22 (top); © Panoramic Images/Getty Images, p. 22 (bottom); © Gerald Hinde/Gallo Images/Getty Images, p. 23 (top); © iStockphoto.com/Eliza Snow, p. 23 (bottom); © Nature Production/Minden Pictures, p. 25 (top right); © Heinrich van den Berg/Gallo Images/Getty Images, p. 27 (top); © Roger De La Harpe/Gallo Images/Riser/Getty Images, p. 28; © Art Wolfe/Stone/Getty Images, p. 31; © Bobby Haas/National Geographic/Getty Images, p. 33; © Tammy Spratt/Zoological Society of San Diego via Getty Images, p. 36; © Greg Seymour/Gallo Images/Getty Images, p. 37; © WILDLIFE/Peter Arnold, Inc., p. 38; © Win McNamee/Getty Images, p. 39.

Front Cover: © Martin Harvey/Gallo Images/Getty Images.

Back Cover: © Royalty-Free/CORBIS.